Original title:
Searching for Meaning While Waiting for Dinner

Copyright © 2025 Creative Arts Management OÜ
All rights reserved.

Author: Natalia Harrington
ISBN HARDBACK: 978-1-80566-178-8
ISBN PAPERBACK: 978-1-80566-473-4

Conversations with the Clock

Tick-tock goes the hand, it's quite a show,
I ask the clock why time's moving slow.
It shrugs and chimes with a cheeky grin,
'Just wait for the chef, let the fun begin!'

Each minute crawls by, like a turtle's race,
I whisper sweet nothings, they vanish in space.
The clock just laughs, oh what a tease,
'It's almost dinner time, wait if you please.'

The Silence Between Courses

The table's set with plates in a row,
Yet here I sit, with nothing to show.
A breadstick crumbles, I toss it with flair,
It lands in the soup, oh, what a scare!

Waiting for flavors to dance on my tongue,
Conversation's quiet, we're still so young.
I poke at my salad, it pokes back in glee,
Oh, dinner, dear dinner, just hurry to me!

Dreaming of Dinners Past

I recall the pizza, oh heavenly slice,
In days gone by, how I'd feast on the nice.
Now I sit here, my stomach a beast,
Imagining pizza, each topping a feast.

Pasta, tacos, all swirled in my mind,
As the clock spins its tales, oh, so unkind.
I beg for my dinner, just one tiny bite,
While daydreaming flavors, I long for the night.

A Feast of Flavors

The air smells of garlic, tomatoes, and spice,
I dance in my chair, oh, isn't this nice?
The salad like confetti, bright colors so bold,
I clap for the chef, who's crafting the gold.

Each second, a course that's just out of reach,
I chat with the napkin, it's quite a peach.
Dinner is coming, it teases my nose,
Oh, the dishes, the dishes, anticipation grows!

Lingering in the Limelight

In the glow of kitchen lights,
I ponder my life's grand heights,
While pasta boils with glee,
I muse on who I'll be.

A spatula in hand, I dance,
Will my soufflé take a chance?
Or will it flop like my last joke,
As I stir the pot and poke?

Dishes of Dilemmas

What to eat, oh what a plight,
To choose between wrong and right.
A curry, a stew, a fruit parfait,
My tummy grumbles, I must say.

The fridge is a treasure chest,
With leftovers that put me to the test.
Should I reheat or let it slide?
Decisions made with kitchen pride.

Soft Footsteps of Thought

In the quiet, my mind takes flight,
Wandering through the evening light.
Where's the bread? Just out of reach,
I'm pondering life while I breach.

Tomatoes sit there, ripe and red,
With veggie friends, they raise my dread.
Will this salad win my heart?
Or will it be a bland depart?

When Aroma Meets Absence

The aroma drifts, sweet and bold,
A story of flavors yet untold.
But my stomach growls in despair,
As if the meal forgot I'm there.

I sniff and sigh, the clock ticks slow,
Maybe it's time for a pizza to go?
Or am I dreaming just a bit?
Oh, the irony of waiting for it!

Recipe for Realizations

Chopping veggies, thoughts collide,
A dance of flavors, can't decide.
The clock ticks slow, my stomach's growl,
I ponder life, with every howl.

Garlic sizzles, dreams ignite,
A sprinkle here, a dash of plight.
Is mashed potato the answer true?
Or just a side for a heart so blue?

Tomato sauce through life's grim strife,
Who knew dinner would cause such rife?
In the saucepan, hopes do stew,
While I wait for forks to guide me through.

So here's my dish, both sweet and sour,
A laugh will rise, in this strange hour.
With every bite, I taste despair,
Yet wonder if it's love or air!

Tantalizing Thoughts

Pasta boiling, swirling wide,
Like thoughts that dance, they twist and slide.
Each noodle bends, a memory spun,
What's meaningful? It should be fun!

Waiting for sauce to thicken fast,
Tick tock, my patience does not last.
A sprinkle of whimsy, a dash of flair,
Wishing for wisdom in the kitchen air.

Cheese awaits, a melty bliss,
Like happiness, what did I miss?
Fork in hand, I make a choice,
Is it the food, or my inner voice?

When table's set and laughter's served,
I find the truths that life has curbed.
In every munch, a giggle pops,
Dinner's here, let's end the stops!

The Cravings of Contentment

In the oven, treasures bake,
As I ponder every mistake.
A burnished crust, golden brown,
Yet here I sit, my muse a clown!

Beans are simmering, thoughts run wild,
Like a restless, hungry child.
Can soup bring solace? Grind my thoughts?
Or just remind me of what I've fought?

A sprinkle of salt; life's bitter tease,
What makes me smile, what brings me ease?
Dinner rolls rise, but so do fears,
In the waiting, I shed small tears.

With butter melted, dreams can glide,
In every bite, let joy reside.
While I chew on life's bizarre quest,
I find my giggles, truly blessed!

Preludes of the Plate

Spoons are stirring, tales unfold,
In every pot, a story told.
Bubbles rise like anxious thoughts,
Where's the meaning? Oh, I'm caught!

Chopping onions, tears roll down,
Frying life's faults, I wear a frown.
Yet laughter's seasoning shouldn't delay,
As rice cooks on, in a silly way.

Garlic's scent, sharp and bright,
Life's conundrums, a comical sight.
What's for dinner? Will it appease?
Or simply tease, with culinary breeze?

As plates are filled with joyous splatter,
I find life's truths, amidst the clatter.
Dinner's served, and humor thrives,
In every bite, my spirit dives!

In the Stillness of Flavor

The clock ticks loud, the pot hums soft,
Hunger's a beast that seems to scoff.
I stare at noodles, they dance in glee,
My stomach grumbles, oh, please feed me!

The spices whisper, a cooking tease,
Garlic and onion, oh how they please.
As time crawls by, my mind takes flight,
Imagining feasts in the pale twilight.

The Taste of Anticipation

A spoon in hand, I gravely ponder,
Chicken or veggies? I sit in wonder.
The fridge door creaks, a sound divine,
Those pickles and mustard—oh what a sign!

With every whiff, my taste buds cheer,
Each simmering pot fuels my gourmet fear.
The timer beeps like a dirge for the meal,
While I'm trapped in thought, oh what a steal!

Feast of the Mind

What if dinner's just a cruel mirage?
A salad of dreams and a burger collage.
Imaginary fries! Oh, how they entice,
But all I have is this cardboard slice.

Reality bites as I chew on my thoughts,
Discussing my options—should I call the shots?
Should I mix up the ketchup with old peanut butter?
At this point, would it even matter?

Twilight of the Table

As the sun sets low, my patience wears thin,
Counting the minutes, I grumble and grin.
Dinner's a dance, a delicate waltz,
While I consider the nature of my faults.

But in this limbo, there's laughter to share,
With every bizarre snack laid out with flair.
So bring on the pasta, the rice, and the stew,
Let's feast on the giggles while we await too!

The Art of Waiting

The clock ticks loud, I stare at the pan,
My stomach growls loud, it's part of the plan.
Each minute drags like a long, boring joke,
Hoping for dinner, or maybe, some smoke.

The dog's got his nose, not leaving my side,
He knows what's coming, he's ready to ride.
I ponder my life, where did I go wrong?
Was cooking a choice, or an old, silly song?

A noodle that's soft, a sauce that's just right,
I daydream of feasts that will dance in the night.
How long till I feast, this anguish I bear,
I check the oven, hoping it's almost there.

I ponder my fate over last night's old fries,
In tinfoil so crumpled, like sad little pies.
As hunger hits harder, I do what I must,
I'll fix up a meal before I turn to dust.

Crumbs of Curiosity

A glance at the fridge, half-opened wide,
Could someone be hiding the food that I bide?
The leftovers whisper, their flavors entice,
But more like a puzzle, not quite so precise.

In the pantry's dark corners, I scavenge around,
Discovering treats where stale snacks are found.
I question my choices, is dinner a myth?
Should I settle for chips or a cold pizza pith?

A pot on the stove starts to bubble and pop,
Could it be magic, or just soup that won't stop?
My questions are many, methods unclear,
I'll eat what's delivered, or at least, persevere.

The dog jumps around, both hopeful and spry,
I'm sure he's a chef in a doggy disguise.
Another five minutes, I check with a sigh,
Just me and my hunger, my thoughts flying high.

The Palette of Patience

Like a chef without spice, I wait for the stew,
Each whiff in the air is a dream overdue.
The timer mocks gently, with each passing tick,
Is this gourmet magic, or just a cruel trick?

I scribble my thoughts on a napkin so neat,
Ideas for dinner, yet nothing to eat.
Do I bake or do I broil? My options seem grim,
While my stomach's a-wailing, oh how we'll both brim!

A carrot and onion, they dance on my board,
And remind me of days when I wasn't ignored.
I stir up the colors, the flavors collide,
But the only creation is my whimsical pride.

The clock strikes again, it's a comical plight,
As I ponder my choices and eat what's in sight.
A feast for my thoughts, just a platter of glee,
While I fish for a meal that's eluded me free.

Breadcrumbs of Reflection

Amidst the crumbs scattered, reflections abound,
Dinner can wait while laughs whirl around.
The oven is glowing, yet humor's my meal,
I'm chewing on moments, I hope they reveal.

As I pace in the kitchen, an artist at play,
A sprinkle of chaos brightens my gray.
There's nothing more funny than timing in life,
Except maybe dinner, or impending low strife.

Why does dinner take ages? I start to suspect,
That laughter is seasoning, it's liberate wreck.
So I whip up a chair, just to sit and to muse,
As the microwave hums with its last tiny blues.

Inhaling the scents, my heart starts to cheer,
These breadcrumbs remind me of savoring here.
So I toast to the waiting, the joy it has lent,
As I pester the pot for a blend that's content.

The Art of the Appetizer

Cheese on a platter, what a delight,
I nibble and wonder, is this dinner or night?
Crackers like canvases, crunchy and bold,
I chew on my thoughts, as the sour turns gold.

Might I dip veggies in hummus divine?
As a painter of flavors, I'm lost in design.
Each bite a distraction, a whimsical play,
As seconds tick by, how long till buffet?

Musing with Morsels

A breadstick's a wand, casting spells in the air,
I wave it around, like I just don't care.
Olive oil pools, a potion to sip,
I ponder the meaning behind this great trip.

Peppers are spicy, jalapeños ignite,
They dance on my tongue, a fiery delight.
Each morsel whispers, as I laugh with my meal,
"Is dessert on the way? How can I steal?

Palette of Pondering

On this colorful plate, I muse and I poke,
What's the flavor of life—a joke or bespoke?
Carrots crunch sweetly, like laughter at play,
While my mind wanders off, it drifts far away.

A bubble of soup, a splash of allure,
I sip and I smile; is that friendship or lure?
In this tasty abyss, I sip, munch, and roam,
Each bite brings me back, I'm still far from home.

Forks in the Road

A fork in the road, or just in my plate?
Decisions weigh heavy, but dinner can wait.
I twirl up the pasta, a slippery twist,
Is the answer to life in this garlic-infused mist?

Salad greens whisper, "Have faith in the blend,"
As I toss them about, oh when will it end?
Time waddles along, like a duck in a race,
I chase after flavors, in this culinary space.

Chronicles in the Kitchen

Pasta boils, bubbles dance,
I ponder life's odd chance.
Garlic whispers, onions sigh,
What's the meaning? Maybe pie.

Spoon in hand, I stir the pot,
Is dinner deep or simply hot?
Chopping carrots, with a grin,
I muse if wisdom's found within.

Timers beep, sauce splatters bright,
I wonder at the cosmic plight.
Are veggies vessels of the soul?
Or just a way to fill a bowl?

Dinner really takes its time,
Life's a joke; I'm the punchline.
Bring the fork and plate, oh dear,
Dinner's served, let's end this cheer!

Edible Echoes

Frying pans and doodles fly,
Bacon sizzles, pants too tight.
What's this flavor? Must be hope,
Or maybe just an olive soap.

Spices whisper, flavors clash,
I finger dip, I take a dash.
Life's a feast of mislaid dreams,
Are chips and dips more than they seem?

I taste a mint of memory,
Wrapped in foil, a mystery.
The avocado's trendy vibe,
Is it wisdom or just a bribe?

Jokes on me, the oven beeps,
While I laugh, my tummy weeps.
Dinner's here, oh what a thrill,
Just another clumsy meal!

A Nibble of Nostalgia

Cookies crumble, memories blend,
I seek a snack, my only friend.
Brownies wink from the tray there,
But what's the meaning? Do I care?

As I munch on chips, I sigh,
Remembering my grandma's pie.
Life's a recipe, so unclear,
Maybe snacks will bring me cheer.

Jars of jelly lining shelves,
I think of all the childhood elves.
Did they bake or roast a stew?
Or just live on donuts too?

Timer rings, the feast begins,
Friendships forged with messy sins.
Is dinner deep or simply light?
Well, who cares? Pass the bite!

The Unfolding Aromas

Thyme and basil swirl around,
In this chaos, joy is found.
Potatoes wander, awkward guests,
While I ponder life's requests.

The fridge hums a silent tune,
As dinner dreams dance by the moon.
Did I close that jar of cream?
Or just lost track, as usual, it seems?

Sauces bubble, flavors tangle,
In this kitchen, I just wrangle.
Do finger foods hold my fate?
Or do they simply just sedate?

The oven glows, a cozy ember,
While I laugh, I still remember.
Dinner served, let's raise a cheer,
In this madness, love is near!

Nuances in the Napkin

A napkin folds with secrets there,
As I ponder what lies in the air.
Is it the stew or my gurgling gut?
Both seem ready to blow their nut!

With each fold, a tale begins,
Will it end with peas, or just my sins?
I twist and twiddle, seeking a sign,
Did I order roast, or just a swine?

Conversations with the Chef Within

In my mind, the chef spins round,
With pots and pans, making sound.
"Where's that meat?" I call out loud,
"Or are we stuck with just a cloud?"

He stirs a pot, a wink, a grin,
"Just add some spice, let's begin!"
But as I wait, I start to think,
Is dinner late, or have I blinked?

Echoes of the Hungry Hour

Tick-tock goes the kitchen clock,
My stomach's growl, a hungry shock.
Should I wait for bread, or take a chance?
Would cheese and crackers lead to a dance?

Echoes sound in the empty room,
Is it dinner time, or just my gloom?
I question if I ordered a feast,
Or if the chef has turned to yeast.

The Balance of Flavor and Thought

I juggle flavors like a clown,
As thoughts come tumbling, upside down.
Should I demand a taste test here?
Or quietly hum, and sip my beer?

With each minute, my patience wears,
Is that a thyme sprig in my cares?
A sprinkle of hope, a dash of fate,
Will dinner come before it's late?

The Palette of Patience

In the kitchen's glow, I sway,
With pasta dreams, I laugh and play.
The clock ticks mockingly, oh so slow,
Garlic bread whispers, 'Time to go!'

Onions dance, their scent is bold,
As I ponder life and tales retold.
A pot simmers softly, bubbles arise,
I crack a joke, and time defies!

The salad toss is quite the chore,
Each leaf a riddle, I can't ignore.
A sprinkle of humor, a dash of zest,
I wait for dinner, but I'm quite blessed!

With every stir, my mind takes flight,
Cooking's a canvas, colorful and bright.
I snack on hope, a bite of cheer,
As dinner approaches, I sense it's near!

Echoes in the Kitchen

This kitchen echoes with thoughts of old,
As pots and pans weave tales untold.
The timer dings, a playful tease,
While I reason with peas and cheese.

I drop a spoon; it clatters loud,
Beating time like a tiny crowd.
Dinner waits, but I've got jokes,
A chef's delight, with all my pokes!

The fridge hums low, like a lazy tune,
While I revisit snacks like a cartoon.
Chips and dip, oh what a find,
The wait grows long, but I don't mind!

As veggies simmer, my thoughts run free,
With every stir, it's comedy.
Dinner will come; I just can't wait,
For now, it's laughs while on my plate!

The Cleaver of Reflection

With a cleaver in hand, I chop and slice,
Each veggie diced with a wink and a spice.
Reflection's not easy in this busy scene,
But laughter's the garnish, living the dream!

Carrots tumble, rolling away,
They giggle softly, 'Let's play today!'
While onions eye me with tearful grace,
I wipe my eyes, it's a funny place.

The oil sizzles, a hissing song,
As I ponder why things go wrong.
Dinner's a puzzle, but oh so sweet,
In this chaos, I find my beat!

The stove's my stage; I'm cooking up cheer,
As friends wait eagerly, their voices near.
I'll flip the script, put on a show,
For laughter's the spice, don't you know?

Seasoned Thoughts

With each spice jar, I ponder life,
A dash of humor, a sprinkle of strife.
The dinner clock mocks with its tick-tock beat,
Yet here I am, concocting a treat!

Paprika and giggles blend so well,
Each stir of the pot tells its own tale.
I mix my emotions like salad greens,
Waiting for dinner, oh what a scene!

The stove's my mentor, teaching me wise,
As I slice through worries like tender fries.
In laughter, I find the joy that's real,
As dinner simmers, this moment I seal!

So here I stand, a chef with a dream,
With seasoned thoughts and a playful team.
Dinner will come; I'll make it grand,
While I dance with delight, spatula in hand!

A Symphony of Scents

In the kitchen, a pots and pans ball,
Their clanging a concert, a chef's call.
Garlic and onions dance in the air,
While my stomach hums tunes of despair.

Fried chicken waltzes, the broccoli twirls,
Each spice a note in the culinary world.
Time trickles slowly, the clock's cruel jest,
As my patience simmers, far from its best.

Pasta pirouettes, a saucy ballet,
While I daydream of flavors' array.
Belly's a drum, and it beats out a tune,
As I wait for the magic to happen quite soon.

Dinner awaits, like a star at the show,
But my fork is just itching, oh when will it go?
With laughter I sigh, as the minutes unwind,
A symphony's playing, just not on my plate, never mind.

Dinner's Silent Prelude

A pot starts to bubble, a soft serenade,
My stomach's the audience, in hunger displayed.
Chopping and stirring, a race against time,
While mealtime's refrain feels like the world's mime.

The clock ticks away, a rhythm offbeat,
As I ponder deep thoughts, like why can't I eat?
Salt, pepper, and laughter waltz through my mind,
In this dinner's prelude, no joy left behind.

I plot a great feast, envision each bite,
But forks and my patience both share in their plight.
The veggies are plotting, to join in the fun,
While I sit here waiting, my hunger's begun.

Finally the dish, a well-practiced act,
After all of this time, it's a culinary pact.
With a chuckle, I dive in, a grand buffet,
As I savor each flavor, my woes drift away.

Appetite for Epiphany

As aroma arises, thoughts start to fly,
Like bubbles in broth, they drift and they sigh.
What's the meaning of life? I ponder while slow,
As meatballs roll past me—hey, where do they go?

Dinner's a riddle, a savory tease,
While tacos and tandoori just bring me to knees.
I'm flipping through menus of thoughts that I share,
But my growling stomach just doesn't seem fair.

O, the wonders of grub, of spices and cheese!
I muse as I wait, with a kind of unease.
Will my heart find its answer with each little bite?
Or just another food coma, an infinite night?

So many thoughts in this culinary trance,
As my salad tosses a leaf in the dance.
With jokes in my belly and crumbs on my chin,
It's time for epiphany, the feast can begin!

The Hourglass of Hopes

Time in the kitchen, it's an hourglass dance,
With grains of sweet hunger, a jet-setting chance.
Each tick a reminder of what's in the pot,
And I'm stuck here wondering, "Is it done or not?"

I daydream of dessert, caught in a plight,
While my hopes rise like bread, oh what a sight!
Tantalizing whispers of what's soon to appear,
But all that I have is a bowl (and some beer).

I check on the roast like a detective on scene,
As my stomach puts on an insatiable keen.
Dinner, dear dinner, why're you being coy?
As I wait with my thoughts, like a kid with a toy.

This waiting's a circus, a comedy show,
As I contemplate life through the crumbs I know.
With forks ready poised and hope in my heart,
I laugh through the hourglass, soon all will depart.

In the Shadow of the Oven

Beneath the glow of warm embrace,
I wonder if I'll find my place.
The cookies bake, the timer ticks,
My thoughts are stirred with silly tricks.

The pasta bubbles, pasta dreams,
Dried herbs dance with hopeful gleams.
As garlic simmers, fate's afoot,
Just when is dinner really put?

The cat, he plots with steely eyes,
A daring heist, no food denies.
While I, a chef of idle thought,
Debate if pizza's best or not.

All while the oven hums along,
My stomach sings a dreadful song.
A culinary quest in vain,
I laugh at all this dinner pain.

Time on My Palate

The clock ticks slow, like molasses,
Hunger strikes, but patience passes.
I juggle plates of what might be,
As whims of flavor dance with glee.

Is broccoli a veggie muse?
Or carrots like a dubious bruise?
Each morsel mocks my idle jest,
While dinner waits, I ponder best.

The fork debates its mighty fate,
Should it serve salad or just plate?
I sip the air, it smells divine,
Yet waiting's not a friend of mine.

As moments stretch like lazy cheese,
I daydream of exotic trees.
A feast awaits, yet here I sit,
In funny thought, I can't commit.

A Recipe for Ruminations

One cup of hopes, a sprinkle of laughs,
Mixed gently with the quickest gaffes.
A dash of dreams in boiling broth,
Will dinner bring the truth or froth?

The chopping board, my therapist,
I slice through doubts, then twist and jest.
What if the roast critiques my style?
Will dinner laugh or just beguile?

A pinch of mayhem, shirt amiss,
The spices dance, oh what a bliss!
Yet all this stirring, what's the score?
Am I a chef or something more?

In chaos found, my thoughts intersect,
While vegetables may leave me perplexed.
But laughter bubbles, warmth can thrive,
So dinner waits, and I survive.

The Taste of Stillness

Amidst the quietude of sage,
I ponder life on this strange page.
The oven hums a gentle tune,
While time and I, we share a rune.

The countdown's clock—my closest friend,
It offers tales that never end.
A bowl of dreams, a pot of cheer,
What doth this silence really hear?

With every tick, a question booms,
Do sandwiches need fancy rooms?
The bread lays low, the butter glows,
While laughter bubbles, wondering flows.

As aromas rise around the space,
I grin, awaiting dinner's grace.
In heated stillness, joy does sprout,
With every moment, I laugh it out.

Appetites of the Soul

My stomach roars like a lion's heart,
Yet here I sit, a world apart.
Thoughts dance like sugar in my tea,
While I wonder where my dinner could be.

The clock ticks loud, a joke so sly,
Imagining feasts that draw nigh.
A salad's whisper, a roast's sweet song,
Why does this wait feel so very long?

As I ponder why some snacks should stray,
Chips in a bowl, leading my brain astray.
The oven hums a lullaby tune,
Why isn't dinner arriving soon?

Belly growls grin like a cheeky friend,
It's hard to think when will this end.
Lost in the whims of garlic and spice,
How is it fair to dine on just rice?

The Clock's Quiet Grumble

Tick-tock, says the clock on the wall,
It might be time for a foodies' brawl.
Jokes of hunger spin like a wheel,
Is that pasta boiling? I can only feel.

With each second, anticipation builds,
Cooking aromas lower my shields.
The fridge hums a whimsical tune,
Could it be dinner at the next moon?

Imagining sauces that might just sing,
While I'm stuck here, a starving king.
The potato peels laugh as they fly,
Yet my plate remains empty, oh me, oh my!

Why does time seem to stretch and wriggle?
I could make a salad, but what's the giggle?
Dinner, dear friend, do find your way,
Or I'll end up tasting my own dismay.

Plates of Reflection

Here I sit with a fork and a knife,
Pondering the meaning of culinary life.
Shiny plates gleam with hope and doubt,
Where on Earth did dinner run out?

With every minute, my mood starts to sway,
Thinking of things that I might say.
A rogue meatball bounces in my mind,
Chasing the thought of what I could find.

The visage of broccoli haunts me so,
Did I ask it softly to join the show?
Or was it the garlic rolling in fright?
Waiting for dinner could spark a delight!

Soon enough, they say joy, not just food,
But waiting can twist my semi-good mood.
Oh, to munch on the whims of this night,
Let the feast begin, and let it be right!

Whispers Between Courses

Between the courses, the jokes emerge,
Like whispers from the fridge on the verge.
Baked potatoes channel a sly debate,
As I contemplate my dinner fate.

Sweet peas giggle while corn gives a wink,
"Will we be served? Let's not overthink!"
The croutons tease with their crunchy dance,
While I'm here wondering if I'd take a chance.

The soup shivers; it's hot, it's bold,
Yet I'm left waiting, growing cold.
Garlic bread sends echoes that softly creep,
But all I want is a bite; don't make me weep!

Waiting is tasty, they say with a smile,
Until I've counted each passing mile.
Dinner's a puzzle, a cosmic joke,
I'll surely eat soon, but we all must poke!

Culinary Curiosities

In the kitchen, pots start to clang,
Where the pasta loops like a circus dang.
The fridge hums tunes, a cooling ballet,
While I wonder if stew will dance today.

Chopping onions, I shed a few tears,
Chef's hat on my head, facing my fears.
A dash of salt for flavor, they say,
But will it taste like gourmet buffet?

Spices whisper secrets in a jar,
These little bottles take me near and far.
Do they know I'm just a home-bound cook,
Creating masterpieces by sheer luck?

Dinner's a show, the ultimate play,
With every ingredient a role to play.
The timer dings, my heart takes a leap,
Did I forget something? Oh dear, I'll weep!

The Simmering Soliloquy

As the soup simmers, I ponder life,
Wonder if I should take up a knife.
Chopping is easy, just dice and slice,
But it's harder to know if it tastes nice.

The oven beeps like a quirky friend,
I seek the joy, but will it all blend?
Garlic and thyme are waltzing around,
Will my dinner be lost, or gourmet bound?

The recipe's gibberish, a foreign tongue,
As I mix and stir like I'm still so young.
Does five minutes mean five minutes, or more?
If only it came with an instruction score.

Guests will arrive, their bellies will growl,
I laugh at my apron, a whimsical towel.
Will they adore my culinary flair,
Or wish they'd chosen a place to spare?

Morsels of Meaning

The table is set, a feast divine,
But how come oil's now starting to shine?
I flip through my notes, pages so curled,
Wondering what joy in between is unfurled.

The roast is dancing, oh what a sight,
Should I give it a turn? It looks just right.
A pinch of this, a sprinkle of that,
What was the point? I just want to chat.

Veggies are scattered like thoughts at dawn,
As flavors mingle, I wonder what's wrong.
Is dinner a quest, or just fuel for the day?
While I wrestle with whims that seem to stray.

The clock ticks loud, I'm waiting in line,
For the moments to stir, divine and benign.
As laughter fills up where silence once sank,
Is the secret of life just a good protein flank?

Ambrosial Anticipation

In the oven, something is whirling,
While outside it's bright and the world is twirling.
Will dinner be bliss, or a culinary flop,
A chance to eat well or just a funny stop?

Flavors collide, a comedic affair,
With each chopped veggie, I'm aware of the dare.
Will they love my concoction, be lost in delight?
Or turn into critics, causing culinary fright?

I glance at my timer, it's been far too long,
Should I freestyle the sauce, or follow along?
The whisk starts to tango on the bowl's side,
While I try to disregard my kitchen's pride.

At last, the hour, guests gather round,
The aroma of garlic, a symphonic sound.
Here's a taste explosion, a flavor so bright,
Will they declare me chef, or flee in fright?

Beyond the Kitchen Door

The scent of spices fills the air,
Belly grumbles, oh what a scare!
Time crawls like a snail on a track,
I peek again - will it be snack?

Mom's in there, humming a tune,
Chopping veggies, it's a cartoon.
But my patience is wearing thin,
Where on earth is that longed-for din?

I pace the tiles, count the ants,
Do they know the dinner dance?
Each tick of the clock adds to the tease,
Can we order pizza, pretty please?

Beyond the kitchen door, I plot,
An escape plan for a tiny tot.
Will I survive this stomach plight?
Oh, the dinner will be worth the fight!

Anticipation Stirring

The pots are bubbling, what a sight,
Watch me hover, like a satellite.
Chop, chop, chop, the sound is sweet,
Just a little longer, I'll have a treat!

Count the seconds, one, two, three,
Each tick mocks my hunger's plea.
Should I set the table with glee?
Or just stand here, dream of my spree?

I suddenly recall that cabbage stew,
Last week, it was like eating glue.
But this time there's garlic in the mix,
Could that turn it into a fix?

Dinner's still just out of sight,
I'm an actor, putting on a fright.
In this comedy of hunger's game,
I'll eat whatever, it's all the same!

The Unseen Feast

Behind the door, a banquet waits,
But here I stand, controlled by fates.
What lies in pots? A hidden lore,
Beyond my reach, oh cruel kitchen door!

The clang of forks is music sweet,
As I imagine each tasty treat.
A roast so tender, or maybe pie?
My stomach sings, a hungry cry.

Sounds of laughter, a clatter or two,
Is that dessert? A scoop or a brew?
I create a menu in my head,
While daydreaming of buttered bread.

The clock moves slow, it's bringing lows,
As I dance around on my hungry toes.
Those unseen platters build my glee,
Hurry up, before I'm a starving bee!

Gazing at the Glimmering Table

Set with colors, sparkling bright,
A feast for kings, what a delight!
I'm a gnome, peering at the scene,
With hopes for meat, or maybe greens.

Oh, the joys of a waiting game,
With every tick, the hunger's lame.
Shiny silverware, napkins like clouds,
If only I could feast with crowds!

A puff pastry in my dream,
Breezes blow with a savory theme.
What will they serve? A wild surprise?
To eat or not - that is the prize!

The dinner bell rings through the hall,
Suddenly, I'm not waiting at all.
I'll feast like a king with every bite,
Oh, glimmering table, it's dinner night!

Banquets of Belief

As pots rumble with a clatter,
A chef's dream sizzles, food to matter.
I ponder life, a salad's grace,
While chunks of meat begin to race.

The fridge hums tunes of distant past,
Leftovers dance, oh what a cast!
I muse on fate while bread is toasting,
Who knew my dinner's worth boasting?

With forks in hand, my thoughts take flight,
On what's for dinner, this endless night.
As veggies whirl and simmer slow,
I question all, a wise veggie show.

The table's set, my heart's in bloom,
Will life unveil a sudden boom?
Behold the feast, it's quite divine,
And here I am, just counting time.

The Taste of Time

I stand by pots, the clock ticks loud,
While sauce bubbles just like a crowd.
What is life but pasta shapes?
With butter dreams and many tapes.

The garlic's scent, a fragrant muse,
I consider all, then hear the blues.
Is dinner here? I check the stove,
While ponderings lead me to the grove.

A chef's cap sits upon my head,
Imagining realms where food is spread.
Yet here I am, still waiting slow,
For flavors deep and soup that glows.

As napkins fold and plates await,
I toast to whims, while swaying fate.
With every stir, my hunger's near,
A comedy of tastes, I cheer!

Flavorful Fleeting Moments

The cheese begins its grand ballet,
As chips whisper, 'Come out and play.'
In sauce-stained dreams, I sit and think,
What drink would match antsy pink?

The potatoes hum a quiet tune,
While carrots conga under the moon.
I chase a thought, what could it mean,
To savor life like nachos keen?

Each minute feels like dough that's rising,
With garlic bread, my thoughts are surprising.
As timers beep, I laugh in glee,
Dinner's near; what's next for me?

Between the waits, my thoughts collide,
In jumbled joy, I cannot hide.
For every dish that's served with flair,
Brings me the gift of laughter's air.

The Elusive Essence of Dinner

In kitchen chaos, pots collide,
With spices dancing side by side.
I wonder what the world will show,
As chicken simmers, time feels slow.

Beneath the steam, ideas play,
Each stir a thought that drifts away.
Like seasoning on life's great dish,
I ponder things I never wish.

The salad tosses dreams anew,
While pepper shakes like it's a zoo.
Each tick of time a playful jest,
In pursuit of flavors, I feel blessed.

As plates unite in joyful cheer,
I laugh with friends, the end is near.
For in the wait, I find delight,
The essence stirs, the stars ignite.

Culinary Contemplations

In the kitchen, I pace with glee,
Hoping for pasta to set my mind free.
Dancing with spices, a twirl and a taste,
Dreaming of feasts that never go to waste.

A pot starts to bubble, it calls out my name,
Is that dinner I smell or just my own fame?
With each little boil, my thoughts take a flight,
Maybe the universe tastes better at night.

The fridge opens wide, a smorgasbord's there,
Leftovers whisper, "We're ready to share!"
I ponder the carrots, the peas with a grin,
Who knew such decisions could stir up within?

With noodles a-simmer, my stomach does sing,
What's life but a cook-off? Oh, let the pot swing!
While my dinner's not ready, my mind's in a race,
To discover the meaning of sauce on my face!

Whispers of the Simmering Pot

A pot on the stove sings a bubbling song,
In my mind, I debate, is this right or wrong?
Should I add some garlic or perhaps just thyme?
As the steam fills the air, I ponder in rhyme.

With a fork in my hand and a colander near,
I question the cosmos, "Why am I here?"
Each noodle I swirl tells a story profound,
While the veggies just giggle, all round and all browned.

Tick-tock, the clock mocks my culinary wait,
Should I whip up a salad or just fry up some fate?
I taste-test the butter, a creamy delight,
While pondering life's purpose in dim kitchen light.

Finally, the timer brings a happy chime,
Dinner is done! What a glorious crime!
As I devour my meal, I realize with glee,
Tonight's greatest lesson was just being free!

Reflections in a Soup Bowl

Peering in broth, it mirrors my soul,
With carrots and onions, oh, what a goal!
They simmer and bubble while I reminisce,
About life's little flavors, both savory and bliss.

Cereal or stew? A question so grand,
Should I stick with the classics or try something planned?

The soup in my bowl seems to chuckle and sway,
As broth becomes wisdom in a funny way.

In the whispers of garlic, I find calm and cheer,
As my appetite ponders the meaning of here.
Each spoonful a journey, each slurp a delight,
What philosophy reigns when all's born of bite?

As I stir the warm liquid, with thoughts all afloat,
I crack a smile at the shapes that life wrote.
Dinner is served, but the laughter's the goal,
Finding joy in the quest, like a taste of the soul!

Savoring Silence

In the quiet of waiting, while dinner does stew,
I consider the meaning of what I must chew.
Dinner's a riddle, each flavor a clue,
What's lost in the oven, what's found in the brew?

With a spatula poised, and a smile on my face,
I ponder the universe, and vegetable grace.
In mixing and mashing, I find sense and laugh,
At the zoodles of life and their curvy sweet path.

Count the minutes like grains of fine salt,
Should I open that door and consult with the malt?
But the casserole beckons from the oven so hot,
Maybe the answers are served on the spot.

As aromas envelop, my thoughts take a spin,
Dinner grows closer; let the fun begin!
In the pause before bites, life seems a grand play,
With laughter the main course, the star of the day!

The Last Grain of Patience

A clock's tick seems louder, what's taking so long?
With every passing second, my stomach sings a song.
The chef's lost in daydreams, or so it appears,
While my fork starts to dance, fueled by hopes and fears.

A napkin becomes a cape, I'm a knight in this wait,
Defending my appetite from hunger's cruel fate.
The oven's a treasure, with gold hidden inside,
But the only thing cooking is my stomach's pride.

As time runs its course, I'm a king on my throne,
Imagining banquets while I'm sampling alone.
A tapestry of flavors, each dish a delight,
But the only thing served up is the appetite's plight.

Finally, there's movement! Could it be at last?
The clinking of dishes, my hopes are amassed.
A feast for the ages, or just endless bread?
I laugh at my journey, the thoughts in my head.

Nostalgic Nibbles

As I wait for my dinner, I glance at the wall,
Pictures of dinners past, they enthrall.
A feast with my grandma filled with laughter and spice,
Now I'm counting the minutes, isn't patience nice?

The scent of the spices, they roam through the air,
Each whiff makes me wonder if I'll be aware.
Of what's on the table, or just what I crave,
Are memories just snacks that we always save?

I'll munch on my thoughts like they're popcorn with flair,

Each kernel a moment, light as candy air.
Dinner's a puzzle, and I'm missing a piece,
A forkful of whimsy for a dash of release.

At last, there's a clang! Could it be time to dine?
But all that I see? Just a slice of sunshine.
So I giggle and grin, with my plate now in hand,
The wait was a journey, oh, wasn't it grand?

Dining with Dilemmas

Sat at the table with thoughts that collide,
Should I dig in now or let patience decide?
The menu's a riddle, a smorgasbord maze,
While my tummy insists it's on fire for praise.

Should I order a soup or a climate change stew?
How does each bite sculpt both my dreams and my rue?
The waiter approaches, his smile like a fright,
"Can I tempt you with choices or just more insight?"

So I ponder my options, oh, the conundrum grows,
With dishes enticing like Shakespearean prose.
The clock's losing patience, I fumble for cheer,
Do I still want the salad, or maybe some beer?

Finally, a plate appears, oh, the culinary sight!
But was it the right choice? Not sure if it's bright.
With each little nibble, I laugh at the game,
Tonight's all about the taste and not the fame.

A Seat at the Table of Thought

Here in my chair, with musings afloat,
The dinner's not ready, but my mind plays a note.
A buffet of ponderings, swirling around,
The feast may be late, but ideas abound!

Why did the chicken cross the lane, I begin?
To ponder the sauce it'll bask in, or win?
The pasta's a plot twist, a mystery too,
Each bite tells a story, of how and of who.

A salad of thoughts layers up in my head,
As I analyze flavors that linger unsaid.
The carrot's a philosopher, the lettuce a sage,
Constructing a banquet but stuck in a cage.

The door swings wide open, is that dinner's parade?
Where each course is laughter and the drinks are homemade.
So I put down my musings, let the laughter ring,
For the best part of waiting is the joy it can bring.

Spoonfuls of Solitude

A pot of water starts to boil,
I chop and stir, my patience toil.
The clock ticks slow, my stomach groans,
I hum a tune, speaking to bones.

A spatula winks, it wants to dance,
But all I can do is stare askance.
The cat's judging me from the shelf,
As if waiting's easy for anyone else.

Sniffing spices with a hopeful grin,
Wondering why it's such a sin.
To think and ponder meals eternal,
While I battle this pot's infernal.

Dinner loves to play hide and seek,
It laughs at hunger with a squeak.
I'll plate the laughter when it shows,
For now, the waiting's all that grows.

The Evening's Expectation

Dinner hovers, just out of reach,
Like wisdom taught on a sandy beach.
I pace and ponder around the stove,
While my culinary fate's still unproved.

My apron's tied, a makeshift cape,
In this kitchen, I'm still aape.
Slicing onions, making a scene,
I'm a chef or a hapless queen.

Bubbling sauces, they wave and shout,
As the scent of garlic winds about.
I pour a glass to ease my plight,
But glass is empty, the meal's a fight.

Tick-tock echoes my growing despair,
I hear my stomach's sarcastic air.
But laughter dances in oven light,
Bringing joy to this arduous plight.

Simmering Sentiments

A bubbling brew, like dreams on hold,
Whisking emotions, both shy and bold.
I toss in hopes, a dash of regret,
Wondering if it's all worth the fret.

Fried thoughts mingle in sizzling glee,
As I wait for this pot to agree.
A minute here, a minute there,
Fried onions laugh, the clock doesn't care.

Count the minutes or count the sheep,
My culinary secrets I try to keep.
With each tick, my plans start to fray,
Will dinner ever come, or just delay?

A spoon's serenade, a fork's sweet song,
In this kitchen, I feel I belong.
With laughter served on a platter of fun,
I'll savor the chaos until it's done.

Delayed Delight

The oven hums a teasing tune,
While I crank up the forks' cartoon.
Timers beep like quirky cheers,
As I avoid kitchen's hidden fears.

Potatoes bubble with eager dreams,
As I plot out savory schemes.
But oh, the pasta plays coy tonight,
Hiding away, out of my sight.

Plate by plate, I fill the air,
With laughter mixed in a crazy flare.
Dinner delays, but who can frown?
When each moment's a clown in a gown?

So pour the wine, let's elevate,
These moments spent, however late.
For what's a meal without some cheer?
Just laughter served, that brings us near.

Breadcrumbs of Insight

Crumbs scattered on the floor,
Morsels of wisdom I explore.
Each bite delayed, my thoughts take flight,
In the realm of hunger, I ignite.

My stomach growls like an old dog,
While I ponder life, lost in the fog.
The clock ticks slow, tick-tock, tick-tock,
I dream of feasts, a banquet to clock.

Parmesan clouds above my head,
A sprinkle of herbs, all thoughts misled.
With every whiff, my brain's in a spin,
The scent of basil, where do I begin?

Gazing at pots that bubble and roll,
Each simmer a question, a hungry soul.
Tomorrow's leftovers dance in my dreams,
With every whiff, my stomach screams!

Plating Deliberations

Dishes lined up, but none on my plate,
My gourmet thoughts, a twisted fate.
What goes with mashed? Should I really care?
As the steam rises, I'm stuck in my chair.

Fork poised high, I'm caught in a plight,
Do I slice, do I sauce, or just take a bite?
The salad's green with envy, I hear it squeak,
My stomach protests, like it's on a streak.

Is tonight the night for tacos with flair?
Or a noble roast that just isn't there?
Balancing flavors like juggling a clown,
While my belly rumbles, and thoughts tumble down.

The wine sits silent, it winks with a grin,
A toast to decisions that just won't begin.
Plating's an art, but my hunger's the boss,
In this culinary chaos, I might come across!

Waiting for the Whispering Oven

Oh oven of wonder, please be my guide,
As I wait for the magic you hold inside.
A warm, gentle hum, like a lullaby song,
While my stomach taps rhythm, oh, what could go wrong?

The timer ticks softly, it teases my fate,
A symphony plays as I contemplate.
Will it be pizza or perhaps a stir-fry?
Or just burned toast that makes me cry?

I draw pictures in grease spots on the floor,
While metaphors simmer and flavors explore.
Whispers of garlic beg me to stay,
While visions of tastebuds wander astray.

O oven so coy, with your bellyful charms,
I dream as you work, my crude little alarms.
I'm twiddling thumbs, as the clock drags its tail,
In this dance of hunger, I hope I prevail!

Dish of Dreams

A plate full of whimsies, my mind goes to town,
While daydreams of pasta help soothe me down.
A sprinkle of chaos, sauce glimmers bright,
Oh, the possibilities, a culinary flight!

Shadows of spices swirl in the air,
While I hum old tunes, no need for despair.
A taco parade or a curry gone wild,
Each thought I abandon, my hunger beguiled.

With spaghetti as ladders and fondue as gold,
In this kingdom of dishes, my love will unfold.
Forks are my subjects, they cling and they stab,
As I wait for the mixer, that magical slab!

Dinner draws near, on the edge of my seat,
Will it land in my lap, or just taste like defeat?
Tonight's the night for the grand debut,
With a plate full of dreams, it's all up to you!

Palate of Purpose

In the kitchen, pots do clatter,
I wonder if my dreams still matter.
Will tonight's meal show the way,
Or just the same old gumbo play?

The bread's alive, it starts to rise,
Whisking thoughts as pasta flies.
Spices dance, waltzing around,
Is this where my hope is found?

Rummaging through the fridge with glee,
What's the meaning of this brie?
Each bite could hold a story,
Or just more food in all its glory.

As I wait, a pot starts to sing,
Maybe I was meant for seasoning.
With every drip and drop I see,
A life flavored with mystery.

The Lure of the Mundane

Chopping onions brings a tear,
As I contemplate my life's career.
Is cooking art or a daily grind?
The thrill of slicing helps unwind.

A cluttered counter reveals my fate,
Juggling dishes and the weight.
Frying stories, sautéing dreams,
I stir the pot and sip my creams.

Countdown ticks, the clock doth chime,
Am I wasting precious time?
Yet here I stand, smock askew,
Questioning why and if it's true.

Loaf of bread, a crusty rhyme,
Mixing laughter in my thyme.
As each ingredient finds its role,
I find a hint of my lost soul.

Stirring the Soul

Bubbling pots with a chatty tone,
Teaching secrets I've never known.
As garlic fries and onions weep,
I wonder if my heart will leap.

In the chaos, things may burn,
But isn't life all about the turn?
The salad's crisp, a crunchy cheer,
Amidst the dice of doubt and fear.

It's comical how a fork can speak,
Reminding me that I'm not bleak.
As pasta twirls in a saucy dance,
I ponder all my lost romance.

Dinner's near; my troubles fade,
In every bite, life's joys cascade.
In this kitchen, I feel alive,
At last, I know how to thrive.

Aroma of Questions

Oh, the scent of burnt toast floats,
Mixing with my wildest hopes.
Does a meal stamp out the blues?
Or simply gives us more to chew?

Diced tomatoes and herbs collide,
With every chop, I'm more tongue-tied.
Sauce bubbles with a mischievous flair,
Is it purpose found in the air?

Waiting for the timer's ring,
I contemplate the joy of spring.
Can recipes hold the key,
To life's great, delicious mystery?

As the oven hums a gentle tune,
My thoughts do waltz around the room.
In this sweet chaos, I can tell,
Every moment's an edible spell.

Messages from the Mixer

Whisking up thoughts in a bowl,
Waiting for something to fill the hole.
A sprinkle of laughter, a dash of cheer,
Maybe this cake will make my doubts disappear.

The hum of the mixer begins to buzz,
Mapping my dreams like culinary fuzz.
As eggs crack and blend, I ponder and stir,
If only my life were as sweet as this pur.

The timer ticks down, or is it just me?
Counting my mismatched socks with glee.
Chocolates and icing are one thing I trust,
While figuring out why my soup turned to dust.

Sifting through life, it's fluff and it's flour,
I'll find my zen in this doughy power.
So, let the dinner simmer, just take a break,
With thoughts like my pasta, I'll twist and I'll bake.

Tastes of Tomorrow

In the oven, my dreams start to roast,
Flavorful wishes, I cherish the most.
Stirring up hope with a pinch of fun,
Wondering when dinner will finally be done.

The fridge hums a tune of potential delight,
As I contemplate life till it's ready to bite.
Slicing through boredom like soft butter spread,
Makes me regret all the snacks that I've fed.

A taste of excitement, a dash of fear,
As I dance with the spatula, dinner draws near.
Each simmering thought flavors the night,
By the time it's all ready, I'll be quite a sight.

But alas, the countdown continues with cheer,
Each whiff of garlic brightens my atmosphere.
I'll toast to my dreams, they're spicy and warm,
As I wait for my feast to take culinary form.

Reflections and Recipes

Chopping away at my tangled mind,
Underneath the surface, I'm trying to find.
A dash of humor, a slice of fright,
Mixing my metaphors, what a delight!

Bubble and boil, the pot starts to sing,
I ponder the nature of everything.
Is that a pinch of wisdom I see in the broth?
Or just last week's leftovers? My thoughts go in froth.

With herbs of distraction and seasoning doubt,
I sprinkle my worries and let them all sprout.
The table is set for both feast and for thought,
Dinner's a canvas where lessons are taught.

So as sauces converge and my mind starts to race,
A recipe flourishes with each silly face.
I gather my answers, one spoonful at a time,
While hoping the meal pairs well with my rhyme.

Serving Up Soliloquies

On the stove of my thoughts, I braise and I bake,
Inventing monologues for dinner's sweet sake.
A platter of ponderings garnished with glee,
Dishing out laughter with each funny spree.

The simmering pot bubbles, my confidence grows,
While I stir up reflections on life as it flows.
Is that a soufflé of wisdom or just my old stew?
Each bite brings me closer to something that's true.

The timer's reminders are witty distractions,
As I ponder my fate through culinary actions.
A taste of the surreal, dessert on the side,
These soliloquies served with humor and pride.

Dinner's a canvas where flavors align,
While pondering life one spritz at a time.
So bring on the meal, let's savor the fun,
With laughter and spices, our hearts become one.

Waiting for the Main Course

My stomach growls with a mighty roar,
A plate of dreams I wish to explore.
The waiter shuffles, a jester's pretend,
While pasta dances, the clock's a fiend.

Brought a salad, a cruel tease in sight,
Lettuce whispering, 'Just wait for the bite!'
My fork is ready, my palate awakes,
Yet here I sit, amidst bread and bakes.

The ambiance hums, like bees in a hive,
As I contemplate why I even strive.
A friend distracted, scrolling his phone,
'We'll eat soon,' I say, 'I'm no longer alone.'

But soon my hopes begin to fade slim,
As the sweet smell rises, our laughter seems dim.
I dream of sauces, of flavors to chase,
Yet here I am, lost in time and space.

Dishes of Destiny

An appetizer winks, we flirt and tease,
But where's the main act? I'm begging, 'Please!'
The menu seems endless, a riddle to crack,
As I ponder the odds of future snacks.

A bowl of soup with very few chunks,
I sip while questioning all of the flunks.
'Is the chef on break, or just having fun?
The coffee's all gone—oh, when will we run?'

My stomach plays tunes like a carnival ride,
As I daydream of burgers, the heart's great pride.
But here comes a plate, with noodles that twirl,
I nearly trip over, my excitement unfurl.

The waiter approaches, but where's my delight?
A smile anticipates what hides on the height.
One more minute, I shout, with a grin—
Dinner's a game, and soon I will win!

The Minutes Turned to Hours

Tick-tock says the clock, but what does it mean?
Each second lingers like an awful routine.
The bread grows cold as we laugh and we wait,
'Will it come before I turn into bait?'

Conversations flutter like leaves in the breeze,
While hunger pangs rise like temperatures tease.
A glance at my buddy, who's snacking for now,
My eyes plead to servers—oh, bad karma, wow.

My watch is a villain, conspiring, I swear,
Every tick draws dragons devouring flair.
Water refills like the hopes in my chest,
'This meal's a quest, will we pass the test?'

And just when despair paints my plate in gray,
Behold the dishes—the trumpets do play!
I holler in triumph, my wait turns to cheer,
Dinner's a saga, and now I am here!

Grains of Reflection

Counting rice grains, one, two, and more,
It's a culinary clock that I didn't adore.
A salad's departure, like lost hopes afloat,
While forks tap softly, we contemplate fate's rote.

The soup's a philosopher, dripping with wisdom,
Each ladle unravels existential schism.
A crusty old roll whispers tales of the past,
While I gnaw on patience, will dinner come fast?

A butterfly flits by, to join in my wait,
'Who knew food could morph into such bait?'
The candle's a witness to all of my schemes,
As I napkin-doodle my food-inspired dreams.

Finally, a savor, a dash of delight,
With laughter combined, we outshine the night.
I muse on this journey, through hunger and jest,
Dinner's a riot; we all are blessed!

Wondering Over Warmth

My tummy rumbles loud and clear,
With thoughts of meals that soon appear.
I check the clock, it mocks me so,
As time moves slow, just like my dough.

The cat's conspiracies unfold,
As I recount the tales of old.
In saucepans, dreams begin to swirl,
While my fate hangs on a garlic whirl.

Should I sneak a bite, or does that break,
The sacred vows I vowed to make?
Each tick a tease, each pang a chant,
The oven hums a hungry rant.

But wait, oh joy, my phone does buzz,
Food pics sent, just because!
I laugh and sigh, what fun it brings,
Imagining meals that make me sing.

The Absent Tablecloth

Dinner's ready, or so they say,
No tablecloth to dress the tray.
Instead, I sit with paper plates,
And forked thoughts on dinner fates.

My neighbors play their nightly game,
Of who's got what, but it feels the same.
I stir the pot, with perfect glee,
Wondering if friends will dine with me.

The cat is judging, from the side,
As my culinary skills collide.
The pasta twirls like it's on cue,
While I just napkin-twirl in blue.

As minutes slip, I forge a plan,
With every spice, a hidden hand.
The missing cloth is now a crown,
In this mad kitchen circus town.

Lengthening Shadows of Anticipation

The sun dips low, my heart takes flight,
As shadows stretch into the night.
A pot simmers, with fragrant dreams,
While smiles dance in dinner themes.

Ticking clocks become my friends,
And playful glimpses of the ends.
I ponder pasta's glorious fate,
In hope it's dressed upon my plate.

My inner chef begins to muse,
With little time, let's stir and fuse!
The salad shivers in its bowl,
As voices echo, 'Let's eat whole!'

Finally, clang! The meal is here,
With laughter, joy, and lots of cheer.
The shadows blend, we gather round,
In this lovely chaos, warmth is found.

Sensations in the Steam

Steam rises high, it billows wide,
While my cravings take a ride.
I sniff the air, it sings a tune,
A symphony from pot to spoon.

The future feast, it teases here,
With every bubble, all is clear.
I stir the broth, my apron bold,
As stories of food dreams unfold.

The neighbor's dog starts to prance,
His nose a-tingle, an eager dance.
We share the hype, a dinner duel,
A race between the pot and drool.

At last, the meal is set to greet,
With giggles, warmth, and love to eat.
In mist and laughter, here we stand,
As friends, as family, hand in hand.

A Fork in Time

The clock ticks loud, the pots they clank,
My thoughts drift far, I lose my rank.
A noodle's dance, a pilot's flair,
Should I eat now? Or simply stare?

The fridge hums soft, a siren's call,
Leftover pizza? Might just enthrall.
But do I dare? It's just one slice,
That feels too bold, a roll of dice!

I count each minute, with growing dread,
The salad wilts, the soup has fled.
Where is the chef? Did they get lost?
The hunger grows, it's worth the cost!

A fork in time, I stab the air,
Where's that meal? I need a prayer.
To season thoughts, a culinary quest,
Dinner awaits, oh, be my guest!

Savoring the Silence

Silence reigns, I tap my toe,
The bubbling pot offers no show.
Should I hum a tune, or just sigh?
The cat gives me that hungry eye.

The bread stays warm, a golden round,
I wait for smells, they make no sound.
A tickle, a thought, or was it gas?
The timer's broken? It's such a farce!

I open the fridge, and take a peek,
A condiment parade, it's quite the sneak!
Brussels and peas, they mock my plight,
Where's the dessert? Oh, what a sight!

In silent rapture, I breathe in deep,
As my mind wanders where flavors leap.
Dinner's a game, a delicious tease,
Perhaps I'll nibble on breadcrumbs with ease!

Culinary Contemplations

The clock hands dance like culinary gnomes,
While I brood in my kitchen—where's all the poems?
A roast in the oven, its scent drifts like clouds,
Yet why's my stomach still sending out crowds?

I'll ponder the meaning of thyme and sage,
In a world where chicken's turned into a cage.
Would my pasta break up with its sauce?
Would broccoli ever become a lost cause?

Hot pans and plates, they all sing in glee,
But my hungry belly yells "Hey! Look at me!"
Oh, culinary whims, you tease and mock,
I want some joy, not a minute's tick-tock!

As I whisk away thoughts of sautéing fate,
I brace for the dinner, it's never too late.
With a pinch of laughter, I stir up the night,
In the grand feast of life, I find my delight!

Hunger's Pensive Pause

In the kitchen, a stillness lies,
My stomach rumbles, I hear its cries.
The oven's glow, a beacon bright,
Yet dinner's a ghost, just out of sight.

I look for wisdom in pepper and salt,
Is it too much to ask—for my meal to halt?
The potatoes grow wise, the carrots conspire,
While hunger plays tricks, igniting a fire.

I ponder just how long I can wait,
This silence becomes an odd dinner date.
A cabbage chic, it wears a crown,
As my appetite edges closer to drown.

Oh, hunger's pause, such a tricky dance,
Will dinner arrive? Or shall I take a chance?
With forks raised high, I strike a pose,
In this comedy of waiting, laughter only grows!

www.ingramcontent.com/pod-product-compliance
Lightning Source LLC
Chambersburg PA
CBHW051645160426
43209CB00004B/800